Seeing Beyond
Where You Stand
Through God's Grace

Matt - I pray this book
bless you tremendously.

I declare Deut. 28:1-14
over you & your family in
the Name of Jesus.

Seeing Beyond Where You Stand Through God's Grace

God has big plans
for your life!

* * *

Carlene Sands

Disclaimer

This is a true story. The real names of the characters and exact locations in this book have been changed to protect privacy.

ISBN: 0692886222
ISBN 13: 9780692886229

Edited by Laura and Mary-Create Space
Scripture quotations are taken from the Amplified, New International Version, the New King James Version, the English Standard Version, and the New Living Translation Versions of the Bible.

Dedication

* * *

To my mother: Thank you for having the strength to carry me into this world and for bringing me to America to pursue a better life and for your prayers. I love you.

To my husband, the love of my life: Thank you for listening to my life story over and over, for your kindness and gentleness, and for accepting me for who I am.

To my children: Thank you for being the two little champions you are and for inspiring me to keep going every day. Never forget that I love you, and you are my special angels from God.

To my mother-in-law: Thank you for praying for me and my family, for allowing your son to marry me, and for your continuous wisdom.

I dedicate this book to children born from rape, children who have been abandoned, individuals who are abused, and people living in poverty. You don't have to suffer. Your faith in God can turn your situation around. He can turn you into His masterpiece, like He did for me.

Contents

Foreword

* * *

I HAVE KNOWN MY WIFE for over twenty-three years, and her story is a testimony of how God can take the shattered pieces of your life and create a masterpiece. She has told me, our children, and a few of her close friends the account of her life in Jamaica over the years. No matter how hard she tried to suppress her past, it held her captive and affected how she related to people. But God can take what seems like it was meant to harm you and turn it into good.

In 2016, God delivered her from her past—a product of sexual molestation who lived in shame, hurt, poverty, and abuse. I have seen her transform from a quiet, secluded person to a virtuous woman that is no longer ashamed of the circumstances of her birth and the early years of her life. My wife developed a hunger for God's word and continues to share it with others so they too can apply it in their lives.

Your experiences may not be exactly like my wife's, but I hope that after reading this book, you will be inspired to pursue the dreams and goals that God placed inside of you. Keep in mind that no matter the extent of the circumstances, God can heal all emotional and physical wounds that you have experienced. Believe me; God is waiting for you to give Him the opportunity to fix what you believe is wrong in your life and align you with His divine purpose for your life. The only true success in this world is walking in your divine purpose through God's Grace. Through God's Grace, my wife did it, and so can you!

-Richard Sands

Introduction

* * *

PROPHETIC WORDS FROM MY PASTORS inspired me to write my book. At the beginning of each year, they set forth a vision for members of the church. In 2016, their vision was, "Reset, Reboot, and Renew."

We were told to select a passage of scripture and to meditate on it. I chose Philippians 3:13–14 (Amplified Bible): "Brothers and sisters, I do not consider that I have made it my own yet; but one thing *I* do: forgetting what lies behind and reaching forward to what lies ahead, I press on toward the goal to win the [heavenly] prize of the upward call of God in Christ Jesus."

In June 2016, I went on a vacation to Jamaica, the country where I was born. On the return flight home to Virginia, I had a spiritual awakening. I needed to tell my story. God's messages are meant to be shared with people around the world. My experiences will show individuals who are lost, hurt, or hopeless that with God's guidance, they can overcome past negative events and shine like the sun through His Son, Jesus.

My life had been like the spin cycle of a washing machine. I felt as if I was living in chaos and always tumbling. Now, I'm at peace with myself—and with my past—through God's Grace, mercy, and protection.

CHAPTER 1

Destined to Be Here

* * *

Before I formed you in the womb

I knew you; Before you were

born I sanctified you; I ordained

you a prophet to the nations.

(JEREMIAH 1:5 NEW KING

JAMES VERSION)

MY STORY BEGINS WITH SUE and what I was told openly about her early life. Sue was born in the late 1950s in a coastal town in Jamaica known for its horseshoe-shaped bay.

She is the only daughter of Ramona and Ramona's first boyfriend—a man who went to England to pursue a better life and who never supported Sue financially. Like me, Sue grew up in a hilly, lush, and green farming community about five miles from the coast. She shared a roughly built two-bedroom house with Ramona, Ramona's second boyfriend, two half sisters, and three half brothers.

Slim and full of energy, Sue loved to swim, climb trees, and play with marbles. She spent many of her days on Ramona's farm planting and harvesting ground provisions—West Indians' name for food staples that grow underground, like yams, sweet potatoes, dasheens, and cassavas. Without the ground provisions, Sue's family would have gone hungry.

But here's what I didn't know about Sue until I was eighteen and had immigrated to the United States: Ramona's second boyfriend raped Sue, and I am the product of his sexual assault.

The rape occurred on the farm, in Ramona's absence. At first, Ramona refused to believe Sue. Older family members expressed their shame, anger, and disgust. Ramona tried to terminate the pregnancy by making Sue drink boiled herbs that were natural abortifacients. However, God had a different purpose and plan. Despite Ramona's efforts, Sue, who was thirteen years old, gave birth to me in the early 1970s and did not include my biological father's name on my birth certificate.

One of the female nurses at the hospital offered to adopt me. Sue refused but has always remembered the woman's kindness. For years, Sue prayed and hoped that I would become a registered nurse. My great-grandfather, who was blind, told Sue to report the rape. Sue was on her way to the police station, and Ramona caught her and sent her back home. They never reported Sue's rape.

Shortly after Sue gave birth to me, she started working at the baseball factory in the farming community, sewing the covers on baseballs. At fourteen, she left me with Ramona in the farming community and went to another city in Jamaica to work as a babysitter.

While Sue was working as a babysitter, she attended a home economics boarding school and graduated as a housekeeper. After that, she went to Kingston, Jamaica's largest city, to work for a judge. She cleaned his house and served as hostess for his events. Sue later became a member of his household.

She returned once to our hometown in the farming community for a quick visit when I was three. In 1983, Sue moved to New York to live with her two sons from a relationship with another man that she had met in Kingston.

What about me? I was raised by Ramona, a tall and medium-brown-skinned woman who spoke Jamaican patois (Jamaican broken English). I called her "Momma," like the rest of the children in my family.

"You must have ambition," she said insistently. I didn't understand what she meant until I was eight years old and looked up the word *ambition* in a school dictionary. I was determined to become noteworthy, and I held onto Ramona's words like a prayer.

Ramona's second boyfriend—Sue's rapist— lived with us. I don't remember him treating me differently. He would send me to the store to buy tobacco for his cigars. Sometimes, I'd buy candy with his money and eat it at my great-grandmother's house. In retrospect, I should have seen Ramona's overprotection of me as a sign that something was wrong.

"I worry about you because of the way you came into the world. I do not want anything to happen to you," she often said.

Ramona did not allow me to go to the beach or to play with the children in my neighborhood. During storms, she made me lie under one of our beds so that I wouldn't get struck by lightning. She told me the thunder would go away if I remained completely quiet.

When I asked Ramona where I came from, she stared back at me—a sign Jamaican children know means "stop prying."

"God is your father," she told me on another occasion. I grew up embracing His love.

I never felt evil in my home in the farming community and was never aware of the secret my family was keeping from me. Yet I could not shake my feeling of otherness. I felt like I did not fit in or belong in Jamaica.

CHAPTER 2

My Life in Jamaica

* * *

"For I know the plans I have for

you," declares the Lord, "plans to

prosper you and not to harm you,

plans to give you hope and a future."

(JEREMIAH 29:11 NEW

INTERNATIONAL VERSION)

ELEVEN OF US LIVED IN the house in the farming community: Ramona, her second boyfriend, their five children, a cousin, my two half brothers from Sue's relationship with a man in Kingston, and me. Sue sent my two half brothers with a family member from New York to live with us in the farming community. We were packed like sardines under the same shingled roof, and our little shack seemed to scream for mercy. Every inch of it was trampled on every second of every day, but none of us had the wherewithal to improve its condition.

The house had several holes in its sides from rain beating on the wood. We stuffed old clothes in the holes to keep the wind and rain out—and to prevent people from looking inside. A calendar with a picture of

Jesus hung on an unpainted interior wood wall.

We owned two queen mattresses. The better mattress belonged to Ramona and her boyfriend; other family members shared the ripped mattress with exposed springs. I often slept on the wooden floor on Ramona's old dress that often slipped from underneath me because I tossed and turned in my sleep. I preferred the hard surface to people touching me or rolling into me at night.

Our house had no electricity or running water. We had one kerosene lamp, and I was often sent to a neighbor's house to borrow matches to light it. Our kitchen and bathroom were outside behind the house. We cooked in an open pit over a log fire, setting our pots and frying pans on blocks and rocks. Meals usually consisted of ground provisions and rice, although Ramona tried to add meat, fish, or beans to our Sunday dinners. I often watched her daily struggles to provide a meal for us and saw the pain it caused her. So I never complained about being hungry and ate whatever was available from the fruit trees.

"Make sure you say your grace," Ramona would yell as each of us found a spot in the yard to sit and eat our food. We couldn't afford a dining-room table. I had to eat fast so my "uncle" wouldn't steal the food off my plate or beg me to give him what I had. I once fought him over a boiled dumpling he had taken from me. Tears ran down my face as I threw my plate on the ground and punched him in the hip. Since no one else would stand up for me, I decided to stand up for myself.

Ramona favored her male children. So I wasn't surprised when she shouted at me after the fight was over. She said I could not go to bed until I had washed all the dishes, while she considered whether or not to physically punish me or give me extra chores. Thinking quickly, I bargained with my uncle and promised to give him my next five dumplings if he told Ramona he was wrong and accepted responsibility for the incident. The deal prevented me from being punished and got me out of extra work, but it left my stomach a little emptier.

As well as hunger, my family wrestled with personal hygiene. I bathed outside in the open behind our house in a round, plastic bin, using whatever I could find as a washcloth—even my own underwear or a dirty washcloth. When my family did not have toothpaste and toothbrushes, I cleaned my teeth with baking soda and a dried corn husk. In other words, I learned early to improvise and be innovative.

Ramona gave me chores—such as cooking, cleaning the house, and filling the water containers. Getting our water was my primary chore, which meant walking to the local government-provided water pipes or to the rivers in Richmond. I carried the filled water containers home on my head. We washed our clothes on riverbanks in large plastic tubs we carried on our heads. When we returned home, we hung the wet clothes with clothespins on a metal line to dry.

I helped cook and did my homework on the ground while I waited for our dinner pot to boil. My small hands were nicked from peeling ground provisions that I could not hold properly. My right hand was permanently scarred from a burn I received while frying chicken. To this day, I do not like frying chicken.

I washed our dishes in a metal pan—a task I didn't mind, except for the heavy scrubbing required to remove the black grime from the pots. Cleaning our wooden floors on my hands and knees was the chore I hated most. The red floor cleaner stained my fingernails. We didn't have the money for rubber gloves. I thought covering my hands with trash bags was a good solution.

Ramona disagreed. She thought it was vanity and my way of asserting my maturity. "Do you think you are a woman?" she yelled. No answer was expected. Ramona then hit me repeatedly in my ribs and back with a piece of bamboo stick. I remember opening my mouth to cry, but no sound came out. She stopped beating me when she saw I was hurt. I swear my ribs felt like they had been broken.

More mild beatings were frequent, and running away from them was pointless. Ramona would hit me in my sleep if I avoided her "justice" during the day. She also attacked me verbally, especially when she didn't receive the money she expected from Sue.

"You'll never amount to anything," Ramona said. "Sue is not taking care of you."

Her words meant nothing to me. I never meditated on Ramona's negative words. Instead, I said to myself, "Watch and see." I don't believe Ramona was a cruel or heartless person at her core. She was a woman battling her circumstances, constantly trying to take care of too many people with limited resources.

Ramona's anger was unpredictable. She was kind one day and quick tempered the following day. Consequently, I developed my own special radar, a sixth sense that automatically detected if someone intended to do me harm or good.

My parentage and birth order made me the family misfit. Older family members teased me because I did not know who my father was, and Sue was gone. "Gweh, gyal. Yuh nuh kno yuh fada, an yuh mada nuh wa yuh,"which means this: *"Go away, girl. You don't know your father, and your mother doesn't want you."* Whenever I was teased, I felt unloved and sad. I would sit under the lime tree and ask God if He loved me. I talked to Him until He comforted me and until I felt happy again.

Younger family members were my responsibility to babysit. The adults frequently went out gambling or to parties at night.

One night, our kerosene lamp ran out of oil as I was watching five children. The house was pitch black. All the kids began to cry. I was only thirteen at the time, and I was scared too. I quieted the children by singing softly to them as we huddled on a mattress. Although they finally fell asleep, I did not. I thought something bad would happen if I did. As my heart raced, I ran next door and woke up a neighbor. He told me he would sit on his porch and make sure no one hurt us. I ran back to our house and fell asleep. His protection—or my peace of mind, really— felt like a blessing.

A gray-and-white kitten, a gift from my great-grandmother, was my best friend. I named her Kitty and spent hours under our lime tree petting her, burying my face in her fur, and telling her I wanted to leave Jamaica.

I was lonely, and she was more comforting to me than any human.

Besides Kitty, I had few possessions. Until I was eighteen, I had three dresses, three pairs of underwear, and one pair of shoes. One dress was set aside for church and trips to the coastal town. One dress was for home, and one dress was a backup in case anything happened to the other two dresses. Every school year, I recieved two uniforms that I wore for that year. After my shoes fell apart, one of my aunts lent me a pair for school and for church. Otherwise, I went barefoot, exposing my feet to broken glass, nails, and hot asphalt. People in the farming community called me the "little barefoot girl."

But I owned something far more powerful and loving than wealth, ease, or privilege. I had deep faith in God. With all my heart, I believed He held me in the palms of His hands. And I believed He would show me the way to a happier life.

CHAPTER 3

Molded by God
and School

* * *

And God gave Solomon wisdom and

exceedingly great understanding,

and largeness of heart like

the sand on the seashore.

(1 KINGS 4:29 NKJV)

IN JAMAICA, OUTDOOR WATER BAPTISMS usually take place at around five in the morning, before the day gets too hot. The pastor, wearing a white robe, stands in the river with the candidates taking the sacrament. Church members watch and sing from the riverbank, welcoming those initiated to the community of Christian believers.

I saw an angel in the water during my baptism. The angel cast a white shadow that spread out like a dove across the river and stayed for about thirty seconds. As I watched it, I felt the Holy Spirit, which confirmed my belief that there is a true and living God and that Jesus was risen from the dead. I don't know if anyone else saw what I saw that day, and I have never shared the memory with anyone until now.

When I was eight years old, I was baptized and christened. Ramona took me to church on Sundays and Wednesday nights. The church was green and white on the inside and held approximately one hundred people. I can't say how deep her faith was—or is. But she attended, despite—or, maybe, because of—the turmoil in her life. For me, church was a place of peace, love, joy, and freedom from my daily struggles. As my faith in God grew stronger, I blossomed. God and the Holy Spirit replaced earthly parents in my heart. I talked to the Holy Spirit the way I would speak to a real person.

Sunday school was another pleasure of mine. Reading the Bible and memorizing scriptures became natural to me. I visualized the characters. One story was particularly vivid. Moses' mother defied the Egyptian Pharaoh's order to throw Hebrew newborn boys into the Nile River. Instead, she placed her son in a basket that drifted on the water and was found by Pharaoh's daughter, who felt compassion for Moses and saved his life.

I give all honor to God for my ability to read and write well. "Lord, give us wisdom, knowledge, and understanding," our pastor would pray. I liked the sound of the words, and I'd repeat them to myself.

When I was three or four, I attended the basic- infant school (similar to preschool) that was next to my neighbor's house. The school had unpadded and hard-on-the-bottom wooden benches, and three to four students sat on each bench. Girls wore a navy-blue jumper, a white blouse, and black shoes. Boys wore khaki pants, a khaki shirt, and black shoes.

I normally went home for lunch and ate whatever was there—usually fruit or bread and butter. Once, all I had was sugared water with lime. I did not go back to school that day.

The woman who taught us is still my favorite teacher. She gave me a lot of attention—perhaps because she knew about my family situation. We learned to raise our hands if we wanted to respond to her questions. Every school morning, she asked us about the weather and held up drawings that matched our answers. Always competitive, I sat in the front of the room, where she couldn't miss my arm waving in the air.

I transferred to the all-age school (starts at grade one and ends at grade nine) for first grade and had to walk two miles to get there. The students were from various socioeconomic backgrounds. Many of the wealthy kids had relatives who lived in the United States, Canada, or England. They also had school supplies I dreamed of but could not afford: new backpacks, lunch boxes, and special pencils. My pencils were cut in half so that Ramona could buy fewer pencils. I chose to bring the half with the eraser to school—or to borrow a whole pencil from one of my rich friends.

Mathematics, reading, and spelling were my favorite subjects. A hardworking, focused student, I was called on frequently in class and was told to watch over the other students when the teacher stepped out of the room.

At the end of each school year, we took a reading and math test to determine our class rank. A male classmate and I vied for the two highest slots out of approximately thirty slots. I remembered his mother was upset with him for letting a girl score higher than him in academics. I actually heard her fuss at him, which made me more determined to do well in school.

The all-age school provided a free hot lunch—bulgur and curried chicken back or bulgur porridge—to children from poor families. The kids with juice boxes, chips, and corned-beef sandwiches made fun of the students who required government assistance. But hunger is more powerful than embarrassment. Believe me, I needed the midday meal. Most mornings, I drank hot tea and ate two crackers or a slice of bread for breakfast. I went without dinner when Ramona didn't have enough money to buy food.

Still, I spent four mostly happy years at the all-age school, and I looked forward to attending the primary school for fifth grade. However, Sue upended these plans. She had arranged for me to be adopted by a couple in Mandeville, Jamaica. Sue only knew the couple through a friend in Kingston. They were childless and wanted a daughter.

I had no idea Sue was giving me away before it happened. Ramona and I rode in a bus to Mandeville, a commercial center with elegant nineteenth-century homes and gated communities. My eyes lit up when I saw the house. It had real furniture, a kitchen with a white gas stove, indoor bathrooms, and four bedrooms. One of the bedrooms—it had a queen bed, a lamp, and a dresser—would be mine alone, the couple told me. They showed me their backyard garden, where they grew tomatoes, cucumbers, and peanuts.

Ramona stayed for about three hours. "You must take care of yourself," she said to me on her way out. I was eleven, and I did not fully understand what adoption was.

For the first time in my life, I had plenty of food and my own bed to sleep in. The couple drove me around the community and to the school I would go to that September. They made me Kool-Aid and corned beef sandwiches on Jamaican hard-dough bread. Despite their kindness, I was heartbroken about the proposed adoption. I had so many questions: Why didn't my biological family want me? Had I been a burden to Ramona, just one more mouth to feed in her big family?

I never adjusted to my surrogate parents or new surroundings. About two and a half months later—after crying myself to sleep almost every night—they arranged to send me home. Ramona picked me up and took me back to the farming community. Only as an adult, seven years later, did I realize Sue was trying to give me a better life.

I went to the primary school after all. The school prepared students for high school, so the learning environment was demanding. My attendance was spotty. The school was a five-mile walk each way on roads with potholes, and Ramona often spent my lunch money for school on other family things, like food. Sometimes, I missed two days of school a week; sometimes, I missed five days. Jamaica didn't have officers or social workers who checked on truancies. When I stayed home, I did chores and napped in between them. Surprisingly, my seventh-grade-entrance-exam scores were average. The high school did accept me though. Thank the Lord. Sue sent money for my high school uniforms and school shoes. I couldn't wait to escape the boredom of summer. Something was buzzing inside of me—the feeling of growing up, maybe, or the freedom of stepping out into the world. I had deep faith in God's plan for me.

School administrators placed me in the second of eleven forms, and I immediately wondered what it would take to get into first form—certainly, it would take higher scores on the entrance test. Wednesdays were my best day of each week. I had math, physics, chemistry, biology, English, French, and Spanish. I also had science labs and enjoyed practicing with the equipment. I never had money for textbooks though. Ramona took a lot of the cash Sue sent for school supplies. Ramona's boyfriend used it to gamble and buy beer.

Once, I tricked Ramona and asked her for three days' worth of lunch money and made it last for an entire school week. However, I ended up being absent at least thirty-four days that year.

During class, my friends let me read their textbooks with them. On most days they asked me to do their homework, which meant

I had to bring their books home. Where there's a will, there's a way, right? I always changed a few answers to prevent us from getting caught.

From time to time, I skipped classes, like history and art, and hung out with friends behind the school or at the beach. We talked about what we wanted to be when we became adults. Back then, I wanted to be a scientist or lawyer. I didn't have the money to participate in many extracurricular activities or to attend school soccer games. I did track and field—specifically, 100-and 200-meter sprints—and represented my school at the Jamaican high school track-and-field competition.

I could only afford to take the Caribbean Examinations Council examination (similar to college-entrance exams) in three subjects:

English, principles of business, and Caribbean history. I passed all three exams, one of them with outstanding. In 1989, I graduated from high school and dreamed of immigrating to America.

CHAPTER 4

Take One Step, and God Will Do the Rest

* * *

Behold, I am doing a new thing;

now it springs forth, do you not

perceive it? I will make a way in the

wilderness and rivers in the desert.

(ISAIAH 43:19 ENGLISH

STANDARD VERSION)

IN 1990, RAMONA RECEIVED A letter from Sue stating that Sue had received her green card and had become a permanent resident of the United States. Sue's immigrant status meant she could sponsor other family members who wanted to come to the United States— exactly what I had been praying for most of my life. I was very excited. I picked up my kitten and sat under the lime tree and talked to God. Ramona was also excited. I later found out that she had used the money Sue had sent and married her boyfriend, making the couple eligible for immigration sponsorship. But Sue would never—under any circumstances—petition for the man who had raped her.

Sue filed immigration paperwork for my half brothers, who are fraternal twins, and me. The days leading up to our appointment with the US embassy in Jamaica seemed to go more slowly than any other days in my life. We received our visas without incident or many questions from the immigration officer.

Ramona warned us not to tell anyone about our plans. Jealousy over people moving on or bettering themselves is a cultural thing in Jamaica. Somehow, we kept our secret for a week. I caught her crying on several occasions, and she constantly reminded us not to forget her. "Don't worry. God will keep us safe," I told her. "We will call and write you."

Two days before Christmas, we boarded an American Airlines flight to New York. While it was not the first time my half brothers had been on a plane, it was mine.

A woman wearing a pretty, blue uniform with lots of buttons and a blue scarf tied around her neck said she would take care of us until our plane landed at John F. Kennedy (JFK) International Airport. At the time, I thought every passenger had his or her own flight attendant. I didn't realize Sue had paid for the service.

When the plane took off, I held onto one of my half brother's hands and anything else I could find nearby. Every time we hit turbulence, I thought the plane was falling out of the sky. I kept my seat belt on the entire flight because I was afraid of falling out of my seat. I was also too nervous to walk to the bathroom and too nervous to eat or drink. My anxiety spilled over as we approached JFK. I was afraid of the landing, afraid of a new life in a new country, and afraid to see Sue, whom I didn't know. The flight attendant handed me a warm cloth to wipe the perspiration off my face and arms. She then took her seat, and minutes later, we were on the ground.

We deplaned through a long walkway. I held all three of our passports and a small grip (similar to a small carry-on suitcase). "Welcome to America," the immigration officer said when we reached the front of the passport-control line. He stamped each of our passports with our date of arrival. "Do not go outside the airport," he told us.

As we sat on a bench at the airport, waiting to be picked up, people around us held up signs with passengers' names, but none of them were ours. We heard snippets of patois, which made us laugh. Jamaicans always make their presence known, even in New York.

Crowds of people streamed through the airport. Men and women with gold teeth and gold-chain necklaces. Outside, planes were taking off and landing, and their lights blinked in the darkness. I was fascinated by all the energy around me.

After about twenty-five minutes, a man and woman walked toward us. I recognized Sue because she looked like one of my half brothers. She asked us about our flight. No hugs or kisses followed the awkward greeting. Sue's boyfriend didn't say much, but he seemed friendly.

We drove from JFK to their apartment in Harlem, Manhattan, New York. The city sparkled with holiday lights, and shoppers jammed the streets. My neck hurt from looking up at the tall buildings, although I couldn't see details at night. My half brothers and I remained quiet in the van, overwhelmed by trying to take everything in. I was finally where I wanted to be—in a new home in America.

CHAPTER 5

Finding My Way in Manhattan

* * *

Trust in the Lord with all your
heart, And lean not on your
own understanding; In all your
ways acknowledge Him, And
He shall direct your paths.

(PROVERBS 3:5–6 NKJV)

Sᴜᴇ's ᴀᴘᴀʀᴛᴍᴇɴᴛ ᴡᴀs ᴏɴ ᴛʜᴇ third floor of a five-story, redbrick building in Harlem. I had never ridden in an elevator before, and my palms were sweaty on the way up. A lit Christmas tree, decorated with red and green ornaments and silver garlands, was in the middle of the living room. Wrapped presents were under the tree.

A gold-trimmed mirror hung on the wall behind her couch, and her china dishes were displayed in a brown wall unit. The apartment had a small kitchen, one bathroom, and two bedrooms—one bedroom for my brothers and me, and the other for Sue and her boyfriend.

We ate dinner at the table, with place settings. We joined hands first, and Sue's boyfriend prayed. Sue served rice and peas, curried chicken, roast pork with slices of pineapples, and mixed vegetables, followed by ice cream and Jamaican sweet-potato pudding. We also drank Jamaican carrot juice, made from carrots; sweetened condensed milk; vanilla; and nutmeg. I ate as much as I wanted, and I didn't have to rush to finish my food. No one was going to take it. Everything was delicious. Still, I had hoped for American food, like macaroni and cheese, pot roast, and salad.

While Sue and her boyfriend washed and put away the dishes, my brothers and I watched television. We could never afford a television in Jamaica, and we were thrilled to have one. Sue and her boyfriend sat with us and told us about the differences between life in New York and Jamaica, an icebreaker conversation they used to get to know us.

We celebrated Christmas on December 25. I don't remember the particulars. But I do remember feeling happy, safe, and so thankful to be in the United States.

After Christmas, Sue set rules for living in the apartment. My chores were to clean the kitchen every night and throw away the trash so that we wouldn't get roaches. The television had to be turned off when Sue went to bed. On my first Saturday in Harlem, Sue took me to a Laundromat and taught me how to use the washers and dryers. She showed me which washer to use for comforters and which to use for sheets. "A machine is a machine," I remember thinking to myself, but I kept the thought to myself.

Saturday morning trips to the Laundromat became my regular chore, along with changing the bed linens, cleaning the bathroom, and replacing the floor mats and hand towels. I also had to pick my brothers up from the public school, which was located two blocks from our apartment. Sue couldn't do it because she worked as a nanny until five in the evenings.

She gets frustrated whenever she has to explain directions to me. I quickly pretended to know uptown from midtown from downtown. I wanted her to believe I was a fast learner. Some nights, I worried that I would mess up an important responsibility and that she would send me back to Jamaica. Tears watered my dreams. I reminded myself that weeping only lasts for a moment and that joy usually comes in the morning. But I never found lasting joy or affection in her apartment in Harlem.

Without prelude or noticeable emotion, Sue told my half brothers and me that she had been raped by Ramona's boyfriend when she was thirteen years old and had become pregnant with me. She said it was the reason we hadn't lived with her previously. Her account angered and saddened me, but it didn't completely surprise me. The rape tied so many aspects of my life together— Sue's absence, Ramona's overprotection, and my family's teasing. It explained why Sue suppressed her feelings and why no one ever mentioned my father. What I couldn't—and will never—come to terms with is how Ramona stayed with this man, had children with him, and eventually married him. I can't imagine—or maybe I can—how cruelly abandoned Sue felt when

Ramona didn't condemn her boyfriend. I do not know what Sue thinks because we didn't talk much about the rape again.

During a trip to the grocery store, Sue and I ran into one of her Jamaican friends. Sue introduced me. "This my daughter," Sue said.

"What? You was going on with things. You have a daughter this big?" her friend asked in reply.

Shame and hurt passed over Sue's face. Her friend was shocked that Sue had a baby at such a young age, and Sue didn't share the circumstances with her. I understood that I was a living, breathing reminder of her violation. I wondered if she saw her rapist's face every time she looked at me.

Following the incident with her friend, Sue found fault with almost everything I did.

I walked too slow when we were out together. I didn't clean the apartment properly. I stayed too long in the bathroom. She called to check up on me from work. When I told her I was watching television, she told me to get a job.

Her complaints filled me with self-doubt. "She must be tired of paying for my food and clothing," I said to the empty apartment. "She wants to send me back to Jamaica." How could I find a job? I had no skills. I didn't know my way around the city, and I had only been in the country for about two months.

While running errands with Sue, I had walked past a local college. I decided to walk back to find out how to apply to one of its schools. The woman at the window of the admissions office asked me where I had gone to high school and when I had graduated. She said that all applicants had to take a writing and math test.

I took the test in a different part of the building. After I completed it, an admissions adviser explained the loans and grants the college offered its students. Finally, I had a way forward, a way to become a scientist, lawyer, or something else. Back home, I cleaned the apartment with extra care, washed the dishes, cooked dinner, picked up and fed my brothers, emptied the trash, and washed the dishes again. Sue couldn't help but be impressed by my effort.

After Sue came home and changed clothes, I told her about my application and the available financial aid, my words tumbling out because I had so much to say. Sue stopped me right away. "I'm not going into debt with the government," she said. No more discussion. Hope for my education passed through my hands like a slippery glass and broke at my feet.

Winter in New York was miserable for me. I didn't own a coat (it never got cold in Jamaica). Sue gave me one of her old coats that felt like it weighed a hundred pounds. She saw how uncomfortable I was and took me shopping, yelling constantly for me to "hurry up." At a store on Broadway, she selected a green coat I didn't like but was grateful for nonetheless. Outside the store, I mentioned the stinging wind that whipped through the streets.

She said, *"Yuh bawl fi come to America; si America yah,"* which means this: *"You cried to come to America. See America here."*

The Holy Spirit spoke to me then, telling me that I was responsible for my goals, not Sue. I listened so intently that I no longer felt the cold, and I didn't noticed when the crosswalk signal changed. A woman had to tap me on my shoulder. I thought about Sue's comment about me being in America now and wondered, again, why we were still eating Jamaican food. Dinner that night was chicken-foot soup and ground provisions, which I disliked.

Sue had—and still has—a softer side. After dinner, she called my half brothers and me to a window to watch snow falling outdoors— something we hadn't seen before. The scene was pretty and peaceful. It reminded me of God's Grace.

I turned nineteen that January. My relationship with Sue continued to deteriorate. Jamaican children do not discuss family problems with their parents, so I never talked about my problems with Sue. I heard Sue on the phone with her boyfriend, a female friend, and one of my aunts saying I needed to find somewhere else to live. I came to the conclusion that they all told her not to put me out.

From August 2, 1990, to February 28, 1991, the United States fought the Gulf War, battling Iraq over its invasion of Kuwait. One afternoon when I was alone in the apartment, I watched news coverage of the conflict and the scud missile attacks. The US Army's "Be All You Can Be" advertisement ran during a commercial break, and it seemed to speak directly to me. For years, I had been waiting and praying for the opportunity to bring out the best in myself. I called the toll-free phone number and talked with a recruiter, who asked me the following questions: "How old are you?" "Where are you from?" "Did you graduate from high school?"

I convinced myself that I could do this—that I could join the army. I told him the following things: "I have a green card and a social security number." "I'm in excellent shape." "I ran track and field in Jamaica." "I have my high school graduation papers."

The recruiter laughed but clearly liked my enthusiasm. "Can I come get you around ten o'clock tomorrow to show you the jobs the army offers?" he asked. He also said I need to take the Armed Services Vocational Aptitude Battery (ASVAB) pretest. I did not tell my family about the phone call or my appointment. My future with the military was in God's hands.

CHAPTER 6

Joining the US Army

* * *

He will cover you with his feathers.

He will shelter you with His

wings. His faithful promises are

your armor and protection.

(Psalm 91:4 New Living Translation)

THE ARMY RECRUITER PICKED ME up the next morning. I was uncomfortable buzzing him into the apartment because I was worried that one of the neighbors would tell Sue about his visit. He took me to the recruiting station in Manhattan, where I was introduced to all branches of the military.

If I had based my decision on uniforms, I would have gone with the marine corps: the dress blues, white hat, and white belt looked sharp. At the station, I took the ASVAB pretest. "Not bad at all," the recruiter said after he scored it. "What do you want to do in the army?" I mentioned wanting to be a nurse or lawyer. Then I looked at him boldly and said, "I'd like your job." He smiled. "OK, I'll make sure you get a job like mine."

I took the final ASVAB test at the Military Entrance Processing Station in New York and signed the contract. I returned to Sue's apartment with a glimmer of hope. Certainly, she would be proud of me. "I joined the army today and will be leaving for basic training soon," I said after she came home.

"That's nice," she replied and said nothing else about my decision, but she did tell me to leave her apartment. "Where am I supposed to go?" I asked. "I don't care. You figure it out," she said. She wanted me to give her my keys when she returned home from work the following day.

I previously heard what she said about me on the phone. But I still didn't understand *why* she wanted me gone. But I did what she asked me to do. I never disrespected her or her boyfriend, and I didn't have a boyfriend of my own, so there was no drama from me staying out too late or being involved with a man she didn't like.

The next day arrived. I dropped my brothers off at school and returned to the apartment. I was alone in the apartment. At around ten o'clock, I knelt on my knees in the living room and prayed to God for protection and for Him to send someone to take me into their home. I prayed for about five minutes, sometimes repeating myself, and then I fell off into a slight sleep.

When I was fully awake, I called my high school friend from Jamaica on the house phone and told her that Sue wanted me to leave her apartment. She said I could stay with her in her apartment in Brooklyn until

I left for the army. My half brothers went with me to the subway station. I kissed them and told them not to worry about me. Sue said nothing when I left. She didn't even ask where I was going.

Once I joined the army on June 19, 1991, there was no turning back for me. I brought my little black New Testament Bible that I read daily. I was the youngest of six recruits flying from New York to Fort Jackson, South Carolina. All six airline tickets were given to me, with the instruction that I was responsible for all six recruits reaching their destination. It was my first leadership test in the military, and I passed.

The drill sergeants at Fort Jackson were as tough as the stereotype. Their constant yelling seemed crazy, honestly. They would yell these phrases: "Look straight ahead." "Don't talk." The drill sergeants schooled recruits on military history, traditions, and required classes. We had to complete a one-mile assessment run and ten push-ups, which were easy for me. Succeeding in basic training meant moving fast and managing our time well. Every waking hour was spent in training sessions, fire guard, eating, or sleeping.

I was assigned to the fastest physical fitness running group for female recruits. I felt excited in my running uniform. The first time we took off, I was running so fast, and then I realized I had gotten ahead of the drill sergeant in charge of us.

"Private, you can't pass me," he yelled. "I lead this group." I immediately obeyed but hated being held back. So I asked the drill sergeant if I could run as a road guard. Road guards are allowed to sprint ahead of their formation for scouting purposes or to talk to other guards. During our next run, I was a road guard.

Breakfast followed physical training. The chow hall (the army dining facility) was chaotic, with more yelling from drill sergeants. We stood at attention, then at parade rest, then back at attention, and then moved forward to the food line. Before we could eat, each of us had to sound off with the last four digits of our social security number. I finally had access to American food, and I hated it—at least, the army's version of it. Fresh fruit and juice tasted better to me than runny scrambled eggs and mushy grits.

Designed to turn civilians into Soldiers, back then Basic Combat Training (BCT) was an eight-week course that was divided into red, white, and blue phases. The course taught tactical and survival skills, including shooting, rappelling, and marching.

I was terrified of the white phase, which taught Soldiers how to shoot our M16 rifles. Lesson one was this: it is a weapon, not a gun—although it sure looked like a gun to me. Our basic rifle marksmanship covered the different parts of the M16 and how to clean and carry the weapon. I did not qualify (I hit twenty out of forty rounds on the target) the first day on the range, so I had to go back and try again. I had problems with the M16's bolt release and had to partner with a Soldier who could execute the move correctly. I made it through BCT nonetheless. Advanced Individual Training (AIT) was next, and I couldn't wait to learn more-specific job skills.

CHAPTER 7

Succeeding in the Army

* * *

Fear not, for I am with you; Be

not dismayed, for I am your

God. I will strengthen you, Yes,

I will help you, I will uphold you

with My righteous right hand.

(ISAIAH 41:10 NKJV)

I COMPLETED MY EIGHT-WEEK AIT at Fort Jackson and trained to be a personnel-actions (human resources) specialist. AIT drill sergeants were more caring; they shouted a lot less than BCT drill sergeants. The emphasis was on teamwork. We had to do well as a class, both academically and physically, or no weekend passes. We studied as a group to make sure everyone understood the material. If someone failed a weekly academic test, he or she was tutored by the Soldier who scored the highest on the test.

Mail call was around seven o'clock every night. I never received a single letter from Sue, although my half brothers had given her my address. I called her occasionally and was continually disappointed by how uninterested she seemed in my army experiences.

My first permanent duty station was in Schweinfurt, Germany. I read about Germany in history books at school and wanted to be assigned there. Before I left for Europe, I took a one-week vacation and stopped in New York. That was a terrible mistake. Sue couldn't have cared less to see me, so I stayed with my friend in Brooklyn.

During my two-year tour in Germany, I met lots of people and made lots of friends. I felt a sense of acceptance and belonging I hadn't experienced before. My fellow Soldiers became my family, although I never told them the circumstances that led to me joining the army. I was invited to numerous parties and was usually the person who looked out for everyone else, since I didn't drink alcohol.

My roommate was a religious, slightly overweight (by army standards) woman in her late twenties. She had failed her first physical-training test, so I was assigned to help her. For five consecutive Saturday mornings, we ran the physical-training route, and she improved each time. She passed her next physical-training test.

My unit officers and noncommissioned officers allowed me to take a night course— Introduction to Business Management—at the University of Maryland University College in Schweinfurt. The course made me more determined to pursue an undergraduate degree.

During my tour, I was standing in line at the bank and saw the Soldier in front of me receive a check with at least five zeros from the cashier at the window. I had never seen a check for that much money before, and it got me thinking about money management and about being a good steward of the blessings God had given me.

As promised, I still sent Ramona money and prayed for her. I saved most of my army paycheck each month. When I left Germany in 1993, I had a significant amount of money in the bank.

From Germany, I went to Fort Sill, Oklahoma. My first job there was clerk for the Casualty Office, a position I was told was given to high-potential Soldiers. Besides answering the phone, I conducted briefings; provided regulatory guidance for senior army leadership in Texarkana, Arkansas; assigned casualty officers to work with the families of

Soldiers who had died on active duty; and helped with funeral arrangements for retirees who had died in our geographic area.

In April 1995, I was promoted to sergeant, an honor and a challenge. Making sergeant back then was based on a combination of factors, including academic and military education, physical fitness, qualifying with a weapon, and an interview with the promotion board. As a sergeant, I outranked Soldiers who had spent more time in the army than I had, which caused resentment and gossip.

"Don't let my age or rank fool you," I'd say. "God prepared me for tough challenges." I could tell by their faces that they didn't understand what I was saying.

An army buddy talked me into going to a ladies' night at a local club, and I went with her only to get out of the barracks. While we were standing in line at around ten thirty to get into the club, a male Soldier started talking to her. She turned to his friend, nodded at me, and said, "She is your home girl."

He told me his mother was born in Jamaica.

I said, "So?" I didn't have warm feelings for Jamaican women.

He told me he was born in the Bahamas.

I said, "So?" I wasn't going to encourage him. I wanted to avoid trouble and focus on my military career. A boyfriend wasn't part of my success plan—not even a fellow Soldier.

He asked for my phone number. I gave him the number of the third-floor hallway phone in the building where I lived. He didn't call me for a week. Then he called one day and asked me out on a date.

I only pretended indifference. Honestly, the handsome, kind, nicely groomed Soldier had made my heart beat a little faster, and the attraction seemed mutual. We went to a Chinese restaurant on our first date. Everything he said and did confirmed my first impression. He believed in God, wanted a family, and liked saving money. I trusted him enough to give him my ATM card four months into dating him and have him withdraw money for me. He passed the honesty test.

After our first date, he spent all his free time with me. A justice of the peace in Wichita Falls, Texas, married us six months later. My husband explained American culture, taught me how to drive, encouraged me to take more college classes, and became my personal and professional partner.

Except for a two-year period when we were both drill sergeants, we worked in the same locations. I served as a drill sergeant in BCT at Fort Jackson, South Carolina, and my husband served as a drill sergeant in AIT at Fort Gordon, Georgia.

In addition to US bases, we served for one year in Dongducheon, Korea. God's Grace—and our love—helped us move through the army ranks. In the latter part of my military service, my husband was assigned to the White House Communications Agency, and I was assigned to the Pentagon.

One of the perks of our assignments was special tours of the White House. I met Presidents George W. Bush and Barack

Obama, Vice President Joe Biden, and Jill Biden. My younger daughter was about six during one of the holiday parties Vice President Biden hosted for military families.

"Do you have any cookies?" she asked him, as we were going through the receiving line. He told her he did and that if she waited until he was done taking pictures, they could eat them together. Sure enough, the vice president found her, and they had a cookie together.

CHAPTER 8

The Power of My Changed Mind and Passwords

* * *

And do not be conformed to this

world, but be transformed by the

renewing of your mind, that you

may prove what is that good and

acceptable and perfect will of God.

(ROMANS 12:2 NKJV)

Nothing was more powerful for me than changing my mind and my passwords. I tried to bury the pain of my past in friendships and expressions of emotion, but these actions didn't deliver me from the issues that were weighing me down. In June 2016, I visited Jamaica and was finally able to let bad things go and accept that I can't fix my hurt on my own.

However, to succeed, I had to first throw in the towel, which seems counterintuitive. I had to make a conscious decision to discover God's purpose for my life, seek repentance for destructive behaviors, and open my heart to His Grace. Some people around me embraced my new normal; other people considered me naïve or extreme.

In cybersecurity, people must change their passwords periodically to protect malicious activities from attacking their networks or Wi-Fi, and the same concept applies to our spiritual lives. Praying, fasting, and studying the Bible resets our spiritual lives, gets us in sync with God, and protects us from evil forces.

Shifts in our lifestyles—a new job, a move to a new city, and new people in our inner circles—are directed by God, and we must be able to hear Him clearly. I also learned that I needed to limit access to people because people are not who they say they are. For instance, I had an acquaintance who pried into my past and manipulated me with the circumstances of my birth, which pushed me closer to God. Now, as a disciple of Christ, I obey God's words and love myself, and I'm fruitful and productive. In the past, although I was happy with my immediate family, I relied on people for acceptance and tried to fit in. But now I do and say only what my Father tells me to. In other words, I am no longer looking for acceptance from people because I'm delivered from people through Jesus Christ. I've become a radical person for Christ. I imitate Jesus' principles and surrender to the Holy Spirit.

I know what it feels like to be on the outside looking in. Being a product of sexual assault, I longed for a family to love me when I was growing up. I so badly wanted a mother and father to take care of me. No mother felt my forehead or gave me a hug when I was sick with a cold or the flu. I longed to go to school every day and visualized the classroom on days when I was forced to stay home. Being on the outside looking in strengthened my ambition and drive for achievement.

My faith in God created a happy ending to my story. Not knowing the truth about how I came into the world caused me to mistrust people until I met my lovely and gentle husband. I married a wonderful man and gave birth to my first daughter in 1996 and my second daughter in 2003.

It was by God's Grace and mercy that I was able to give birth to my second daughter. My second pregnancy was painful, and I was miserable. I couldn't hold food down and urinated on myself when I coughed. My assigned doctor kept telling me that nothing was wrong with me or the baby all throughout my pregnancy.

One of my Soldiers told me to skip my regular doctor's visit, and she called and got me an appointment with the head doctor of the obstetrician clinic. During my doctor's visit, I was standing in the hallway at the hospital, and the doctor said, "Come here, Sands." He said he wanted to do an ultrasound to check the baby. His assistant prepared the room, and they conducted the ultrasound. He turned to me and said, "That's what I thought. Your baby is breached." My second daughter was breached at full term.

During the same week, we found out the house we were renting had been foreclosed. I had to get an emergency C-section, and my husband was attending military school. However, God sent people—and angels— to help me. One angel in particular was a woman who came to stay with me in the hospital. After I was discharged from the hospital, she visited me at my home. She made sure that the baby clothes were folded and helped me walk from my bedroom to another room in the house.

My husband also got some time off from his military school. While I was in recovery, my husband purchased our first home. God had turned what looked like a desperate situation into a great situation.

I can attest to God's protection over my family. My daughters love God, and they enjoy going to church. They loved and accepted me despite my story. My oldest daughter is currently a junior in college, majoring in finance with hopes of becoming a financial attorney. My youngest daughter is currently in middle school with hopes of becoming a scientist one day. A scientist or a lawyer was what I wanted to be when I was growing up in Jamaica.

I earned the rank of master sergeant in the army. I earned a bachelor's degree in management from Park University and a master's degree in cybersecurity policy from the University of Maryland University College. I am a fellow in the Brookings Executive Education Fellowship, a fellowship program offered by the Brookings Institution in Washington, DC, and Washington University in Saint Louis.

Today, I'm on the inside looking out. I now have a loving family who grounds and sustains me. I no longer face poverty or abuse. I retired from the army, and I am working for the federal government. I provide financial support to several ministries to help people who are less fortunate.

I will remain humble and open to where God will take me in the future. I will lift up people who are struggling in their personal journeys and put them on a spiritual path. God determined where I needed to be, and my calling is to follow Christ.

ACKNOWLEDGMENTS

* * *

I WANT TO THANK *EVERYONE* who God has allowed me to meet thus far. Your connections with me had an impactful outcome. I've learned, and I've grown. I appreciate your prayers, love, and support, and all the other things that make me cry.

Borrowing the words of Bob Marley, I say that there is "one love," and I say that's God's love.

ABOUT THE AUTHOR

* * *

CARLENE SANDS IS A US Army veteran who was born in Jamaica. She is a member of the Authors Guild. She holds a bachelor's degree in management and a master's degree in cybersecurity policy. She is currently attending the Brookings Executive Education Fellow Program.

Carlene is an active member at her local church, where she serves in the children's ministry. She currently works for the federal government and lives in Virginia with her husband of over twenty-two years and their two children.

Contact Author at carsand72@gmail.com